THE STORY OF

PAUL REVERE
Messenger of Liberty
BY JOYCE MILTON

ILLUSTRATED BY TOM LA PADULA

A YEARLING BOOK

ABOUT THIS BOOK

The events described in this book are true. They have been carefully researched and excerpted from authentic autobiographies, writings, and commentaries. No part of this biography has been fictionalized.

To learn more about Paul Revere, ask your librarian to recommend other fine books you might read.

Published by
Dell Publishing
a division of
Bantam Doubleday Dell Publishing Group, Inc.
666 Fifth Avenue
New York, New York 10103

ISBN: 0-440-40361-8

Published by arrangement with Parachute Press, Inc.
Printed in the United States of America
October 1990
10 9 8 7 6 5 4 3 2 1
CWO

Contents

Paul Revere: Midnight Messenger

Listen, my children, and you shall hear
Of the midnight ride of Paul Revere,
On the eighteenth of April in Seventy-five;
Hardly a man is now alive
Who remembers that famous day and year.
—Henry Wadsworth Longfellow, 1861

Paul Revere's midnight ride was a wild chase on horseback that changed American history.

It happened on an April night in 1775. Massachusetts was a British colony at that time. For more than ten years, groups of people in the thirteen American colonies had been protesting the way they were being treated by England. The protesters wanted to have some say in how they were governed, but the British did not give them any. The colonists did not want to pay taxes when they had no role in making laws for the colonies, or in deciding how the money would be spent.

England had decided to punish the colonists by

1

sending soldiers to Boston. But the rebellious Americans refused to give in. Some of them had begun collecting guns and ammunition. These weapons were hidden in the village of Concord, outside of Boston.

The British soldiers found out about the hidden weapons. On April 18, 1775, the soldiers decided to make a surprise raid. Their soldiers would leave Boston during the night, and capture the rebels and their guns in Concord at sunrise.

It was a good plan. If it had worked, the British might have been able to crush the American Revolution before it even got started.

But the British hadn't counted on Paul Revere. Riding a borrowed horse, Paul raced from village to village that night, waking up sleeping families with the shout "The Redcoats are coming!" The British soldiers were called Redcoats because their uniforms were red. When dawn came, and a thousand British soldiers marched down the road to Lexington and Concord, the people were out of bed and waiting for them.

During the time of the Revolutionary War, Paul Revere was a hero. Everyone in Boston knew the story of "bold Paul." He was famous for his courage, for his skill as a rider, and for being one of the leaders of the fight for freedom.

But as the years went by, Americans forgot about what happened on the night of April 18–19,

2

1775. Everyone remembered the generals, like George Washington. They remembered the political leaders, like John Adams and Thomas Jefferson. But few gave much thought to "bold Paul."

That's how things were until 1825. That was the year when the people of Lexington decided to celebrate the fiftieth anniversary of the Revolutionary War. One of the speakers at the ceremony was an old man who had helped to hide the rebel leaders to keep them from being captured by British soldiers during the war. He talked about Paul Revere's exciting ride.

After that, Paul Revere became a hero again. The famous poet Henry Wadsworth Longfellow eventually wrote a poem about Paul's midnight ride. Longfellow's poem was thrilling. Schoolchildren all over America learned the ringing phrases by heart:

> The fate of a nation was riding that night;
> And the spark struck out by that steed, in his flight,
> Kindled the land into flame with its heat.

But even Longfellow did not know very much about Paul Revere, or about what happened on the night of his great ride. In fact, you may want to read Longfellow's poem which is at the end of this book and see if you can pick out the mistakes that he made.

Today, we know much more about this great

American patriot. Paul Revere was a talented artist, a successful businessman, and one of the organizers of the Boston Tea Party. Even more important, long before most of his countrymen, he had a vision of a free nation called America.

The Silversmith

When Paul Revere was a boy growing up in Boston, his father's workshop was one of the most interesting places in the city. Paul's father was a silversmith. He made spoons, teapots, bowls, and many other items.

Mr. Revere's shop was warm and cozy, even on the coldest winter days. The charcoal fire burning in the brick oven at the back of the tiny shop gave off a cheerful red glow. It was not a fancy place—the furniture in the shop was shabby, and the windows were small and covered with soot. But the customers who came through the door included some of the richest, most important people in town.

Many of these customers brought bags of money with them when they came to the shop. Paul's eyes would open wide as he watched a well-dressed man counting out stacks of heavy, silver coins. But the coins were not used as money. After the customer had gone, Paul's father threw them into a pan and placed it over the fire. Soon the fancy pictures and words stamped on the faces of the coins began to turn blurry and run together. The money was starting to melt! Before long, noth-

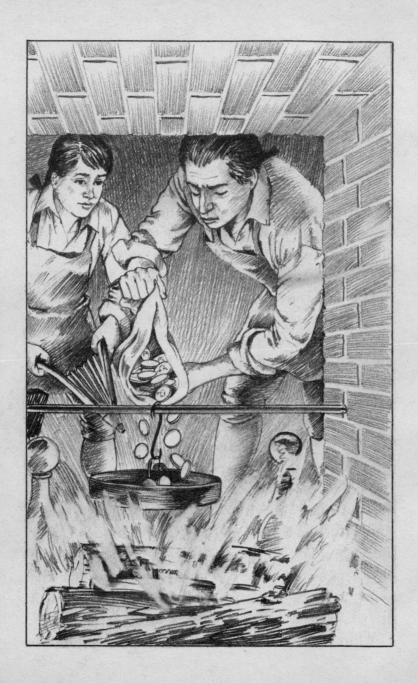

ing was left in the pan but a puddle of liquid metal.

Paul's father watched the pan carefully. At just the right moment, he pulled it away from the fire. Then he added a pinch of special chemical. If for some reason there was any other metal in the coins besides silver, it would stick to the chemical. As soon as this happened, Paul's father carefully filtered out any impurities.

Nothing now remained of the customer's money but a stream of pure silver. Quickly, Paul's father poured the precious liquid into a mold. When it cooled, he could begin to make all kinds of wonderful things.

Most often, Mr. Revere made buckles and spoons and cups. For his richest customers he sometimes made bigger things, such as trays, tall coffeepots, and even punch bowls. These would be decorated with seashells and flowers, or with designs that had a special meaning to the customer's family. From time to time, customers also brought him gold coins to work with. From these, he usually made beads or jewelry.

Paul was very proud of his father. The things he made were useful, and beautiful, too. There weren't many people in Boston who could say that their customers actually paid them to melt down money!

It took a special kind of person to be a good silversmith.

First of all, silversmiths had to be honest. It would have been very easy to pour off a little gold or silver and add cheaper metal in its place. Silversmiths who cheated in this way soon saved enough silver or gold to make fake coins. They would then use other people's silver to buy things for themselves. Sometimes they weren't caught for many years—if ever.

A silversmith also had to be strong and brave. Everyone in town knew that there was gold and silver in his shop. Some people might try to steal the precious metals. For this reason, smiths usually lived in the same building where they worked. When the sun went down, they locked their houses up tight. A silversmith could not afford to be a heavy sleeper. If there was a noise in the street in the middle of the night, he jumped out of bed and ran to the window. He had to be ready to guard his shop against thieves.

Most of all, a silversmith had to be skillful and talented. He had to know how to make dozens of different objects. Most of his customers wanted designs that were different from the ones their neighbors had. A smith hardly ever made two sets of bowls, or two sets of cups, that looked exactly alike. And since the metals he worked with were so expensive, he couldn't afford to make mistakes.

Paul Revere was one of nine children. He had an older sister named Deborah and seven younger brothers and sisters. As the oldest boy in the family, Paul was named after his father, who was also called Paul Revere. From the day he was born, no one ever doubted that some day Paul would take over his father's silversmith business. He was very lucky to have a father who could teach him such a good trade.

Paul knew that his own father had not had such an easy time getting started. The story of how the Revere family came to America was one that Paul and all his brothers and sisters knew well. Paul must have heard it many times while he was around the shop, watching his father work.

Paul's father had not always been called Paul Revere. As a little boy he went by a different name. He was called Apollos Rivoire.

Apollos was born in Europe, in the south of France. The village where his family lived was hundreds of years old, and so lovely it could have been the setting for a fairy tale. From spring through autumn, the countryside was filled with flowers. Even the winters in that part of France were mild.

The Rivoire family was rich and lived in a large, comfortable house with a big garden. They owned land outside the village where they grew grapes for making wine. Apollos was lucky to have two loving parents, and many cousins to play with. He seemed to have everything any little boy could want.

But the Rivoire family had a dangerous secret: They were Protestants.

The king of France was a Catholic, and he had decided that everyone in the country should belong to the Catholic Church, too. Protestant churches were outlawed. Officially, the Rivoires became Catholics—they had no choice. But the family only pretended to believe in the Catholic religion. They kept on saying their favorite Protestant prayers at home. And once in a while, when a Protestant minister was brave enough to come out of hiding, they would hold a secret church service.

When Apollos was born, he was baptized in a Protestant ceremony. This alone was enough to ruin his life in France. If the king's officials found out, he could be sentenced to jail. Or he might be sent into the navy or the army, where the officers would put him to work at the hardest jobs until he died or became too weak to work anymore.

The only way to live safely as a Protestant was to leave the country. So on Apollos' thirteenth birthday, in 1715, his parents decided to send him away. First, Apollos went to live with an uncle on Guernsey, an island off the coast of England. Unfortunately, there wasn't much work on the island, so his uncle decided that Apollos would have better opportunities in America.

Somehow, Apollos' uncle heard about a silversmith named John Coney who lived in the colony of Massachusetts, in Boston. Coney needed an apprentice. An apprentice was someone who worked without pay in order to learn a trade. This uncle had to pay Mr. Coney money for teaching Apollos to be a silversmith. In return, Apollos promised to work for ten years for free.

A few months later, Apollos Rivoire arrived in America. Although he had lived on an island where everyone spoke English, he knew only a few words of the language. Hardly anyone in Boston understood French. But Apollos adapted to his new home. As the years went by he changed his name to Paul Rivoire, then to Paul Reviere—and finally, to Paul Revere. He married a girl named Deborah Hitchbourn, who lived very near the Coneys, and he set up his own silversmith's shop.

The Reveres were an American family now. But Paul's father had not forgotten the reason he had been sent away from his home—so that he could have the freedom to worship in the Protestant church. Since Massachusetts was an English colony, and the king of England was Protestant, just about everyone belonged to one Protestant church or another. There were many churches, and each had its own character. Mr. Revere picked out one of the stricter churches. He went every Sunday, and he took his family with him. Sometimes the services lasted for hours.

The rule in the Revere family was church on Sundays and hard work the rest of the week. But the mood at home was anything but gloomy. The Reveres were a close family, and they were proud of their independence. They enjoyed each other's company. Any outsider who became friends—or enemies—with one member of the family soon found that he had to take on *all* the Reveres in the bargain!

Young Paul was born on New Year's Day, 1735. As the oldest son, he knew that someday he would have the responsibility for being head of the Revere family. He did not mind this at all. But it would take many years to become a master silversmith. Most young men were in their mid-twenties before they took on the work and worries of running their own workshops. In the meantime, Paul was determined to enjoy himself as much as possible.

Bold Paul

North Boston, where the Reveres lived, was an exciting place to grow up. Some of the older houses had big backyards. Many families kept chickens, ducks, and pigs in backyard pens. Often, a neighbor's goose, or even a pig, would escape. Then Paul and all the other children would start running after it. The chase would go on for many blocks before the animal was caught.

There were no streetlights then, so at night the neighborhood was as dark as any country village. As soon as the sun went down, Paul could look up at the sky and see millions of stars twinkling overhead. Candles and lamp oil were expensive. To avoid using more of these than they had to, the whole family went to bed early. And early in the morning, Paul woke to the sound of roosters crowing in the backyard.

Boston was growing fast when Paul was a boy. The crooked streets and alleys bustled with activity. Most people walked everywhere they went, but the rich drove around town in horse-drawn carriages. At the sound of a horse's hooves clattering on the paving stones, all the people who were strolling

down the narrow streets would hurry to get out of the way.

One reason Boston was so busy was because it was a seaport. The Revere house was on Fish Street, just one block from the waterfront. From Paul's front door it was just a short walk to Clark's Wharf. Clark's Wharf was one of the biggest of several piers where ships from all over the world docked to load and unload the goods they carried. Almost every day a big sailing ship came in. Some of these ships brought limes and molasses from the West Indies. The molasses would be made into rum in the colonies, and then shipped off to other parts of the world. Other ships were loaded with goods from England, such as velvet cloth, glass bottles, fine books with leather bindings, and all kinds of tools. The harbor was crowded with fishing boats, too, and their decks were piled high with cod and mackerel. Some of the fish would be loaded into the holds of the big ships and taken back to Europe.

The sailors who worked these ships were often strange characters. They came from all over the world, and they spoke many different languages. During the long weeks at sea, they did not have any chance to spend the money they earned. So when their ships came to port, most of the sailors had lots of coins jingling in their pockets. Food vendors and peddlers crowded onto the wharf, hoping to sell fresh oysters and sweet cakes to the sailors. Musicians played and sang for coins. One animal trainer paraded a tame bear, while another man claimed to have the only talking dog in the colony of Massachusetts!

The wharves were a great place for children to play. And North Boston had plenty of children.

One of Paul's younger brothers, and one younger sister, had died when they were just babies. That left seven children to share the crowded rooms over Mr. Revere's shop. No one considered this a big family, since many other families were even larger. Paul's aunt and uncle, whose name was Hitchbourn, had ten children.

Paul and his brothers, Thomas and John, often played with the Hitchbourn boys, either around Clark's Wharf or on another nearby pier that was owned by the Hitchbourn family. In warm weather the boys tore off their clothes and went swimming off the edge of the pier. They stared at the sailors and watched the ships being unloaded. Sometimes, they ran up a ship's gangplank and started climbing the masts!

Paul's four sisters were not included in most of these adventures. Little girls played near home, and as soon as they were old enough they were given chores to do around the house. Mothers tried to keep an eye on their daughters, but boys had a lot of freedom. They were expected to know how to take care of themselves.

Paul was short and muscular, with dark brown hair and very white teeth. Even when he was very young, he was a leader. He was always a good athlete, and he was never afraid to speak his mind, even around grown-ups. You might think that talking back to grown-ups would get Paul into trouble, but this doesn't seem to have happened, at least not very often. Most adults liked Paul. He was one of those boys who was always busy organizing some project or another.

The Revere boys didn't have *all* their time free. They spent a few hours a day learning their ABCs from a woman who gave lessons in her home. In Boston, children had to know the alphabet before they could even get *into* grammar school. By the time Paul was eight years old he knew his letters and could read simple sentences. He was ready to go on to regular school, where the first thing he had to do was pass a reading test.

Paul attended what was called a "writing school"—its name was North Writing. All the students were boys, and most of them were going to grow up to work at some trade or craft. Boys who planned to go on to college went to another kind of school, called a "Latin school." Latin schools taught Greek, geometry, and other subjects in addition to—what else?—Latin. Writing schools taught mainly reading, writing, and arithmetic.

Even so, North Writing was a hard school. The boys wrote with quill pens, and they were expected to have good penmanship. They recited their lessons out loud. If a boy made a mistake, the teacher might smack him with a stick. It was no use complaining. The teacher's word was law.

Attending North Writing cannot have been much fun, but Paul did not seem to mind. He was considered just an average student. Even though as an adult he would still struggle with his spelling, he did learn to love books and reading. And he could make up poems and funny, rhyming riddles. He may have worked harder than most of his classmates. He also learned enough arithmetic to keep the accounts for his father's shop. Later, he was able to go on to teach himself chemistry and practical science, which were useful for a smith to know.

After five years, soon after his thirteenth birthday, Paul quit school. It was time for him to start learning to be a silversmith.

As his father's apprentice, Paul was soon working six days a week. On Sundays the shop was closed, but it was not a day for playing around. The Lord's Day was supposed to be set aside for church and reading the Bible. Many activities were forbidden.

This does not mean that Paul never had any fun. On holidays, and on special occasions like weddings, there were often parties. Teenagers, and sometimes grown-ups too, played games like blindman's buff. Some boys bragged in their diaries that they used these games as an excuse to steal kisses from—and "tussel" with—the girls.

Even work could be fun. Boys Paul's age were expected to help put food on the family table. They went out fishing and duck hunting. Paul learned how to handle a small boat and to shoot a gun. He also became one of the best horseback riders in Boston.

No one knows exactly how Paul learned to ride. But silversmiths, like his father, often owned at least one horse. Once in a while, they used these horses to deliver goods to their customers. The streets of Boston could be rough. Sometimes thieves were about. By riding a horse, instead of walking, it was easier to make a quick getaway if necessary. Paul may have taken over this important job.

Bostonians were very proud of their horses. In fact, horse racing was practically the only sport that even grown men took time for. Races were planned weeks in advance. The prize was usually a silver medal, ordered from Paul Revere's father or from one of the other silversmiths in town.

The races were held on the beach at low tide, when the smooth sand at the water's edge made a good racecourse. When the big day came, everyone gathered on the beach. All the horses were bunched together at the starting line. Someone fired off a gun, and the whole pack took off at once.

Speed wasn't enough to win these races. A rider had to keep his horse from getting spooked by the noisy crowd and the crashing waves. He had to watch out for rocks and big shells that might cause his horse to stumble. He also had to keep from getting bumped by the other horses. Often it was the most skillful jockey, not necessarily the fastest horse, who carried off the prize.

As a teenager, Paul often went to the races. Did he ever get a chance to ride? Did he win? We don't know for sure, but we can imagine that he did. By the time Paul was a young man he was known around town as an excellent rider. Perhaps racing was one of the ways he earned his reputation.

Paul Becomes a Bell Ringer

The church that the Revere family belonged to was named the "New Brick Church."

Years earlier, the members of the New Brick Church had all belonged to a bigger church called the "New North Church." For some reason, the congregation of the New North Church had started to argue among themselves. Eventually, the losers of the argument left to start their own church. They became the founders of the New Brick Church, which was built right across the town square. When the building was finished they had a huge copper weather vane put up on the roof. The weather vane was shaped like a rooster—or, to use the old-fashioned word that was popular in those days, a cockerel. Because of the weather vane the people of Boston had nicknamed the new church the "Cockerel Church."

On the day "the revenge church" was dedicated, a man from the congregation climbed up on the roof and sat on the copper rooster, waving his arms and crowing at the members of the New North Church as they arrived for Sunday services.

No one in Boston seemed to think that there

was anything especially strange about this behavior. Bostonians were famous for enjoying a good argument. They even liked to argue on their way to church.

The New Brick Church did very well until they hired a new minister. The Reverend Pemberton's sermons were very boring. And he was very fat. The members of the church nicknamed him "Puffing Pem." One member complained of having to sit in her pew and watch him "roll up the stairs" to the pulpit. Puffing Pem was so unpopular that every Sunday fewer and fewer people came to hear him. Before long, the Cockerel Church had hardly any members left.

But even before Puffing Pem was hired, young Paul Revere seemed to have found the Cockerel Church too stuffy for his taste. Paul was the sort of boy who didn't like to miss out on the action, and this applied to churchgoing, too. He began to look for a new church.

One of the churches Paul visited had a minister named Mr. Mayhew, who often shocked his congregation by giving sermons about history and politics. One day, he preached about a time a hundred years earlier when a group of rebels in England rose up against King Charles I. Eventually, the rebels put the king on trial and chopped off his head.

Mr. Mayhew's sermon gave the impression that he thought the rebels had the right idea. He said that self-respecting people would never take orders from a bad king. Everyone listening knew that the minister's words also applied to the current king, George III, even though he didn't say so specifically.

All of Boston was excited about Mr. Mayhew's sermons. Fifteen-year-old Paul Revere was one of the people who crowded into Mayhew's church to hear him preach. Paul's father was angry with him for this. Mr. Revere did not agree with Mr. Mayhew—he felt lucky to be living in a Protestant country. He was loyal to the king of England.

Paul and his father argued about Mr. Mayhew. According to one version of the story, old Mr. Revere won the argument and Paul promised never to go back to Mr. Mayhew's church. Most likely, Paul just pretended to agree. He was a good son, one who didn't look for trouble with his parents. But he was stubborn, too—he never really forgot Mr. Mayhew's sermons. Chances are, he couldn't resist going back.

There was another church in North Boston where Paul spent even more time. This was Christ Church, whose members included some of the wealthiest people in North Boston.

The members of the Cockerel Church did not believe in Christmas decorations or in organ music. They thought these things were too frivolous to be in a church. But Christ Church had decorations galore—and music, too.

In addition to an enormous pipe organ, Christ Church had eight big bells that were famous all over Boston for their musical sound. The biggest bell weighed more than fifteen hundred pounds, and the smallest one more than six hundred pounds. When all eight bells rang together the music was something to hear!

Paul and his friends thought that ringing the bells would be even more fun than listening to them. Six of them formed a bell-ringers club.

Paul and his friends must have enjoyed ringing the bells because they convinced the church to let them have time to practice. For two hours a week, the boys had the bells all to themselves. They would tug on the ropes and make the heavy bells swing back and forth in different arrangements.

In those days the purpose of bells was not just for music but to spread big news to the people of the city. The bells of Christ Church rang for weddings and for funerals. They rang when a ship arrived at the docks with important news from Europe. They rang when there was a fire or some other emergency.

Even though he was still a teenager, Paul had an important job. Whenever anything major happened, he and his friends were among the first to know. The whole neighborhood relied on them to spread the news.

Kiss the Devil

Kiss the devil!
Shall you kiss the devil?

Every year, on the fifth of November, the streets of North and South Boston filled with shouting people. They were celebrating the strange holiday known as Pope's Day, when a group of young men paraded through town, pulling carts containing dummies dressed up like the Pope and Catholic priests. The very last cart in the parade held the tallest and most frightening-looking dummy of all—a figure with horns on its head and a long tail that was supposed to be the devil himself.

In England, Pope's Day was called Guy Fawkes Day. It celebrated the capture of a group of Catholics who had been plotting to blow up the Parliament building in London.

A holiday whose whole point was to make fun of Catholics was a nasty idea, to say the least. But in Boston, people did not think much about the original reason for celebrating November 5th—it had

been all but forgotten. Hardly any of the boys and men who marched in the Pope's Day parade had ever so much as met a Catholic. There wasn't a single Catholic church in all of Boston.

Pope's Day had become much like our Halloween. It was a chance to dress up in scary costumes, parade through the street, and beg for treats from the neighbors. And as with Halloween today, the fun sometimes got out of hand.

By the 1740s, Pope's Day celebrations in Boston had become very rough indeed. The big parade started just after sundown. Since there were no streetlights, many of the paraders carried flaming torches. At the head of the marchers rode a man dressed in black. He was called "Joyce Jr." after a man named George Joyce, who had been the one to arrest King Charles I many years before. "Joyce Jr." was supposed to be a bad character, but the man chosen to play this part was usually someone very popular with the crowd. He was the unofficial king of the parade.

Behind Joyce Jr. came the carts carrying the strangely painted dummies. Boys and young men from the neighborhood followed after the carts, laughing and chanting. Joyce Jr. would challenge the crowd to "kiss the devil." Only the bravest boys had the nerve to climb up onto the devil's cart and give "Old Nick," as they called him, a kiss!

After the parade, there was a big bonfire. The

dummies and all their carts got tossed into the flames.

When Paul Revere was still a boy, the people who planned the Pope's Day parade split into two groups. They formed two separate celebrations. One parade was organized by a club from North Boston, and another by a club from South Boston. The two clubs did not get along. By the end of the night, they were sure to run into each other, and when they did there was always a nasty fight.

Paul had seen his share of Pope's Day parades, but by the time he was nineteen, he was too busy to waste his time on pranks and street fighting. He had more important things to do.

In the summer of 1754, old Mr. Revere died suddenly. Paul took over his father's silversmith shop. The law said no one could be a smith until he was twenty-one years old, so in theory the shop belonged to Mrs. Revere. But Paul was the one who knew how to do the work. No one stopped him from running the shop.

Paul worked hard. With his mother as well as six brothers and sisters to take care of, he was very busy. For almost two years he spent most of his time at the shop, joining in few parades and celebrations. But one day, another kind of parade came marching past his door—one he could not resist. A line of British soldiers led the way, beating out a solemn rhythm on their drums: rat-a-tat-tat, rat-a-tat-tat. Behind them was an army captain, and he paused every block or so to make an important announcement: The colony of Massachusetts needed volunteers to fight the French.

Paul signed up for the army. Immediately he was made a lieutenant. It was a proud day when he marched out of Boston in front of his men. But the fun soon turned into very hard work. The Massachusetts volunteers had to walk all the way to Albany, New York—then north from Albany to the shores of Lake George. There they were assigned to build wooden boats that other soldiers would use to attack the French fort across the lake.

All summer long, the volunteers cut trees and dragged them down to the shore of the big lake. At night, they slept in tents in the woods. The work was backbreaking, and the camp was full of biting black flies. Clouds of these pests followed the soldiers wherever they went. Worse yet, the forest was full of Indians who were fighting on the side of the French.

One day, Paul's men were chopping trees when suddenly an arrow came whistling through the woods. A man cried out and fell to the ground. The others chased after the attackers, but it was no use. The Indians knew too many hiding places. Paul's men could not find them.

The volunteers in Paul's group were mostly city boys. They knew nothing about fighting in the woods—in fact, they were lucky if they could find their way back to their own camp at night. It was a helpless feeling, knowing that they could be ambushed at any time. Almost every day, the Indians killed a few more volunteers. Each man wondered if he would be the next to die.

When fall came, it started getting too cold to sleep outdoors in the woods. Some of the volunteers fell sick. In late November, the order finally came to start for home. Shaking with cold, the volunteers had to march all the way back to Boston—more than two hundred miles!

Paul's duty as a volunteer was finished. He hadn't learned much about soldiering except that he didn't like it. But after months of marching and chopping down trees he looked lean and handsome. He was twenty-one now, and old enough to run the Revere silver shop in his own name. He was also old enough to get married.

A slim, dark-haired girl named Sara Orne lived in Paul's neighborhood. The Ornes belonged to the Cockerel Church, so Paul and Sara had known each other since they were both children. Sary, as Paul called her, had grown into a fine woman during the months he was gone. Before long, Paul was courting her.

Sary and Paul were married the summer after he got out of the army, in August of 1757. By the next spring they had a baby girl. They named her Deborah, after Paul's mother and his oldest sister.

This was a happy time for Paul. He had always enjoyed making beautiful things out of silver, and now he was master of his own shop. The bowls and teapots Paul made were sleek and elegant. His customers saw right away that he had special talent. Even when Paul was still in his twenties, he was known as one of the best silversmiths in Boston.

The family rooms over the store on Fish Street were crowded. Paul's mother lived with him and Sary. So did his brother Tom, who was now Paul's apprentice. Paul's younger sisters also lived at home until they got married. He and Sary, meanwhile, were on their way to having a big family of their own. After Deborah, they had a boy—a third Paul Revere. Then came a girl, called Sara, after her mother.

Paul didn't mind the noise and close quarters of his home. He enjoyed being the head of a big family. When he had a few hours free to get away from the bustle of Fish Street, he used the time to meet more people. Paul soon belonged to several social clubs. He was meeting some of the most important men in Boston—doctors, lawyers, and merchants.

Of all Paul's new friends, his favorite was a young doctor named Joseph Warren. Dr. Warren was a good-humored and handsome man, with blond hair and light blue eyes. Everyone who knew him commented on how clean he was, too. This was unusual. In colonial times, many people did not wash very often, and even doctors sometimes had dirty hands. But not Joseph Warren.

Warren had graduated from Harvard and had very modern ideas. Some of his ideas were thought to be on the dangerous side. For instance, he didn't think that King George III and the English Parliament were treating the thirteen American colonies fairly. And he thought Lieutenant Governor Thomas Hutchinson, who helped run the Massachusetts colony for England, had too much power. Warren and some of his friends even laughed at the lieutenant governor behind his back—they called him "Tommy-Skin-and-Bones."

Many rich people who were faithful to King George were offended by Warren's criticisms. They did not like the fact that Paul was friends with the doctor. A silversmith needed to be on good terms with the rich families in town. Paul's friendship with Warren threatened to cost him business.

In 1763, another crisis occurred that almost ruined the Revere family. A terrible disease called smallpox had come to Boston. Smallpox started with a fever and itchy blisters, like chicken pox. But the disease was much worse than chicken pox. Many of those who caught it died. Others lived but were left with terrible scars. No one knew how to cure smallpox, but everyone understood that it was very contagious. Outsiders wanted nothing to do with people who were sick with the disease. They were too afraid.

Soon there were cases of smallpox in seven houses near Clark's Wharf. One of Paul's children was among the first to get sick. Paul was called before the Board of Selectmen. This is what the people of Boston called their town council, the group of people who made local laws and regulations. The selectmen had decided to send Paul's sick child to a house at the edge of the city. Although this house was called a "hospital," it was nothing at all like a modern hospital. It was just an empty building where the sick were kept out of sight until they either died or got better.

Paul refused to send his child there. "I love all my lambs," he said. He couldn't bear to send one child away to die, even if that might save himself and the rest of his family from catching the disease.

The selectmen were very unhappy. They ordered the whole Revere family to stay shut up inside their house. A big flag was hung outside the door, to warn visitors to stay away. The town even hired an armed guard to march back and forth in front of the house. Paul's shop was closed, too, and no customers could come near it. Kind neighbors left food for the family, but otherwise they were on their own.

The smallpox epidemic killed one hundred seventy people. But the Reveres were lucky. All of them lived.

The Sons of Liberty

T he smallpox was just the beginning of Boston's troubles. Business was very bad. There had been a lot of shipping activity during the war with the French. Now that the war was over, many of the men who worked on the wharves were out of work. Worse yet, the English Parliament picked just this time to try to make the people of the thirteen colonies pay new taxes. In 1765, a new tax law called the Stamp Act went into effect. Certain kinds of papers, including newspapers, had to carry stamps, which cost money. The money the colonists were to pay for these stamps would go directly to England.

The Stamp Act was the beginning of a long bitter argument between England and the colonies. In a way, it was like a family quarrel. The American colonies were growing up. They wanted to have a say in how they were governed. But Parliament, which made the laws for England and all the colonies, did not respect the colonists' wishes. They saw only that the Americans were getting more prosperous. Now that the long-drawn-out war with France was finally over, Parliament wanted the colonies to help pay the bills for the war.

The new taxes were the talk of Boston. In the evenings, after the day's work was done, shopowners and craftsmen would gather at the local taverns to discuss what was happening.

There were many taverns in Boston, and most of them had interesting names. One was called the "Green Dragon." Another was called "Cromwell's Head." The taverns were not just for drinking. Men went there in the evenings to talk about business and politics. Often, there was a back room that was reserved for meetings of a political club. Paul was soon attending meetings of the club at the "Salutation," a tavern not far from his house.

Some of the members of the club that met at the Salutation were what people at the time called "Mechanics"—men who worked with their hands. Others were merchants, ships' captains, and even doctors like Joseph Warren. Paul was a "Mechanic," but he was also friendly with the more educated members of the club. Since he had the respect of both groups, he was a natural leader.

One of the most interesting characters Paul got to know at the Salutation was Sam Adams, the local tax collector. Sam Adams was very bad at his job. Strangely, this was exactly the reason why he was so popular. He felt sorry for the poor, so he made no effort to get them to pay their taxes. The poor thought this was a wonderful way for a tax collector to behave.

For some time, Sam Adams had been worrying

about two different problems. First of all, he wished there were some way for the colonists to show England how much they hated the new taxes. And second, he was concerned about the violence of Pope's Day, which seemed to get worse every year.

In 1764, almost a year after the smallpox came to Boston, the Pope's Day celebration was the worst yet. Several people were killed. Sam Adams decided that the time had come to put a stop to the street fighting. He thought of a way to get the two groups to forget their differences by convincing the leaders of the gangs to join together to fight the Stamp Act. By finding a cause that they both agreed on, Adams had discovered how to solve both his worries!

On August 14, 1765, the people of Boston woke up to a big surprise. Hanging from one of the biggest trees in the center of town were two dummies. They were exactly the kind of figures used during the Pope's Day parade. But now the dummies represented the man in England who had thought up the Stamp Act, and the man in Boston who had agreed to sell the stamps.

A crowd gathered. Everyone wondered where the dummies had come from. Who had been brave enough to hang them up?

At dusk a parade of men came marching down the street and gathered around the tall old elm tree. A drummer was playing the beat for a funeral march. Someone cut down the dummies and put them on a cart. The dummies' "funeral" parade

snaked its way through the streets to the State House, where the governor would be sure to see it. Their message was clear. They wanted an end to the Stamp Act.

"Liberty, property, and *no stamps!*" chanted the marchers. "Liberty, property, and *no stamps!*"

That was how Boston learned that a new holiday had replaced Pope's Day. From now on, Liberty Day would be celebrated instead, every August 14. The old elm tree where the dummies had hung was named the "Liberty Tree." And the former Pope's Day gangs were now called the "Sons of Liberty."

People still referred to one figure from Pope's Day, however. "Joyce Jr.," representing the man who had once arrested King Charles I, was now a name used for someone who was against British rule of the colonies. Bostonians who sided with the English were warned that Joyce Jr. was going to run them out of town. No one knew who Joyce Jr. really was, but his warnings were feared.

Not everyone thought the Sons of Liberty was a great idea. Many of the group's members were tough and wild, and sometimes they got out of control. They threw rocks at the windows of Bostonians who supported the British. Once, a gang of vandals even broke into the house of the lieutenant governor. They broke up his fine furniture, and stole money and jewelry. His terrified family barely escaped out the back door.

John Adams guessed that a third of the people in Boston were still loyal to the king of England and would have been happy to see the Sons of Liberty thrown into jail. Another third of Boston's population didn't care much about politics one way or the other. But the third that supported the Sons included many of the most thoughtful people in town. They saw that the time when England left the American colonies to fend for themselves had come to an end. They were convinced that if they didn't take a stand now, the situation would only get worse.

The Sons of Liberty were rebels, no mistake about it. But they resisted the temptation to kill to get what they wanted. Paul was one of the leaders responsible for keeping order. The attack on the lieutenant governor's house was not repeated, partly because of Paul's influence. Instead, the Sons found other ways to frighten and embarrass those who were friends of the British. Sometimes, they would meet outside the person's house and serenade him with violins. Since few of the Sons really knew how to play, the "serenade" sounded awful—more like fighting cats than music.

Little by little, the Sons of Liberty became more organized. The members wore special caps and medals that they hung on leather thongs around their necks. They practiced marching and planned parades.

When Parliament canceled the Stamp Act, in

May of 1766, the Sons held their biggest celebration yet. The main feature of the parade was a huge decorated tower made of oiled paper. The tower was covered with cutout designs of such things as an angel, a Liberty Tree, and even a mocking picture of King George III. These designs were lit up by three hundred oil lamps that fit inside the hollow tower.

The tower of lanterns was the brightest, most spectacular display of lights anyone in Boston had ever seen. It was considered so amazing that the town fathers even let debtors out of jail for the evening to see it!

The Sons of Liberty had planned to end the celebration by parading the tower through the streets. But before the procession really got started, the wonderful tower caught fire and burned up. Disappointing as this was, the Sons considered "Illumination Day" a big success.

Naturally, the English did not agree. Parliament was determined to show the people of Boston that they would have to pay taxes whether they liked it or not. It soon passed another law, calling for taxes on certain things, like tea, that were brought into Boston by ship. The taxes on these things would have to be paid before the ships could even be unloaded.

The plan seemed foolproof, but in Boston it didn't work any better than the Stamp Act had. The officials who were supposed to collect the taxes on the docks were so afraid of the Sons of Liberty that they hardly dared show their faces in the streets. They didn't succeed in collecting a lot of the money they were supposed to. They and their families actually moved to a fort located on Castle Island, out in the harbor. There, they would be safe from attacks by the Sons of Liberty.

In the meantime, many people had taken up smuggling. This was the docking of ships and unloading of their cargo in a sneaky way, so the tax collectors wouldn't know anything about it. Even John Hancock, the richest young man in Boston, became a smuggler. Hancock had become the owner of Clark's Wharf. When ships carrying smuggled tea, glass, and other items docked at the wharf, the workers found ways of sneaking the cargo off the ships.

Paul Revere found his own method of contributing to the cause of liberty. Few people were ordering silver in these troubling times, so he took up a new trade—engraving. In the days before photography, engraving was a way of making copies of pictures. The engraver used a sharp tool to draw deep lines on a copper plate. By rolling ink on the plate, a printer could use it to print the same picture over and over again.

Paul's engravings were a lot like the political cartoons that appear on the editorial pages of newspapers today. One of them made fun of seventeen Massachusetts politicians who had taken sides with the king of England. It showed the seventeen men being herded away by a group of devils. The title of the drawing was "A Warm Place—Hell." This was exactly where Paul thought Americans would end up if they let the king of England order them around.

Paul Learns Another New Trade

One day in 1767, a ship from England brought a stranger named John Baker to Boston. Mr. Baker's luggage was filled with strange objects: hippopotamus tusks, animal teeth, gold and silver wires, carving tools, and even a few heavy iron tongs that looked like instruments of torture!

Mr. Baker was a dentist, the first ever to visit Boston. Before he came to Boston, Mr. Baker had been a dentist in London and in Ireland.

In colonial times, most people did not take care of their teeth. If a tooth started to go bad, there was nothing to do but let it rot. When the rotten tooth was loose enough, its owner would start looking for someone to pull it. Rich men and women usually went to their doctors, while the poor got their barbers to do the job. A few people even went to blacksmiths!

Mr. Baker soon learned that Americans had even worse teeth than the English or the Irish. No one really knew why. Some colonists thought there was something wrong with the air in America; they believed "bad air" made teeth rot away. More likely, Americans had problems with their teeth simply because they ate a lot of sweet cakes and molasses candy!

Mr. Baker did not know how to save decayed teeth by filling cavities, the way dentists do today. But he did know how to make false teeth. Soon he had more customers than he could handle.

Since the silversmith business was so bad, Paul Revere was looking for new ways to make money. He started taking lessons from Mr. Baker. Even though Paul had never studied medicine, he was soon in business as a dentist.

At first, Paul specialized in making new front teeth. The best false teeth, or dentures, were carved from whale or hippopotamus tusks. Sometimes, though, Paul would use gold or silver—or even real teeth from sheep, elk, or other animals. Paul used gold wires to attach the dentures to the patient's own teeth.

Within a year, Paul was making complete sets of false teeth. The top and bottom teeth were held together by metal springs. The springs were so strong that, if the owner wasn't careful, when he started talking, his false teeth would come flying out of his mouth!

Unlike dentists today, Paul made house calls. He cleaned and scraped his patients' natural teeth. He sold his own brand of toothpaste, although he didn't call it that. The formula for Paul Revere's tooth cleaner was a secret. Probably it was a powder made of chalk dust, with ground-up coral or even tiny pieces of broken dishes added. When the powder was mixed with water, these rough bits helped scrape food and dirt from the teeth.

Did Paul like being a dentist? Chances are he didn't. As soon as he no longer needed the money, he gave it up.

A year after Mr. Baker arrived in Boston, other visitors who were *not* so welcome came from England. One day, in September of 1768, eight big ships sailed into Boston Harbor. The ships belonged to the British Navy. They were loaded with two regiments of soldiers, about six hundred men in all, sent by Parliament to make the people of Boston behave.

The British soldiers wore splendid uniforms of white trousers and long red jackets. They were professionals, not an organized street gang like the Sons of Liberty. On a Saturday, two weeks after the soldiers arrived, they left their ships and marched through the streets to show Boston what a real military parade should look like. Drummers and flute players led the way. The soldiers stood up tall and marched in straight lines.

Now that the soldiers had arrived, the Sons of Liberty didn't dare hold any more celebrations. No more dummies were hung from the Liberty Tree. The officials who had been hiding on Castle Island moved back into Boston. With the soldiers to protect them, the officials no longer had to worry about their own safety.

Everything seemed peaceful, but many people in Boston were bitter. They resented the fact that Parliament had decided to send an army to frighten them, instead of listening to their complaints.

Boston did not like the troops, and the troops did not like Boston. Little boys followed the soldiers, making fun of their red coats. "Lobsters!" the boys called them. And worse, "Bloody Backs!" Some of the soldiers were rude—they pushed people around and even took things from the stores without paying. But it wasn't easy for them to do their job, either. It could be dangerous for a soldier to stand guard alone. Teenaged boys teased them and tried to make them lose their tempers. Sometimes the boys threw stones and oyster shells.

One cold winter night in 1770, well over a year after the soldiers had arrived, the situation got out of hand. Although it was early in March, there was a foot of snow on the ground, some of it having fallen that morning. For the town boys, new snow was an invitation to pelt the "lobsters" with snowballs. Over on King Street, where a group of soldiers were living, a sentry got tired of being teased. He punched a teenaged boy.

Within minutes, a big crowd gathered. The mood of the crowd was ugly. Several people threatened to attack the sentry. "Kill him!" one voice called out.

The frightened sentry decided to call for help.

47

"Turn out the guard!" he yelled. "Turn out the guard!"

Eight more soldiers came running. Their leader, Captain Preston, ordered them to load their guns.

Everyone could see that there was going to be trouble. Some of the more sensible people in the crowd started urging the others to go home. But a number of the young men were excited and angry. They thought Captain Preston was just bluffing. They were sure the soldiers' guns weren't even loaded.

The crowd started pushing and shoving. The sentry got knocked down. "Fire!" a voice ordered.

Shots rang out. Five men and boys fell down. Three of them died immediately. The other two were so badly hurt that they died soon after.

Within hours, news of the shooting was all over town. People called it "the Boston Massacre." Thomas Hutchinson, the lieutenant governor of Massachusetts, ordered that the soldiers be charged with murder. No one doubted that they would be found guilty.

Within hours of the Massacre, Paul had made a drawing that showed where the victims were standing when they were shot. A few days later, he started engraving other pictures of the scene. Four of these engravings appeared in a Boston newspaper, the *Gazette*. Copies of another engraving went

on sale three weeks after the shooting. The "lobster" coats of the soldiers were colored in with red ink. The blood of the victims was colored in red, too.

In the meantime, some Bostonians were starting to ask questions about the shooting. Why had there been such a big crowd on the streets that night? Who had hollered out the order to fire? Was it Captain Preston? Or was it someone else? One story told was that "Joyce Jr." had been making a speech nearby, whipping up the crowd to attack the soldiers. A few people even wondered if Sam Adams hadn't planned the whole thing.

At first, there wasn't a lawyer in Boston who would defend the British soldiers. But finally, two attorneys named Josiah Quincy and John Adams agreed to take the case. Both of them were very much against Britain, and for that matter, John Adams was Sam Adams' cousin. But both lawyers believed in justice. The soldiers had a right to be fairly represented. When the case came to trial, they argued that the soldiers had fired in self-defense.

At their trial a few months later, the jury agreed. The nine soldiers were found not guilty of murder.

There was still a lot of anger over the Massacre, but Boston was proud of the verdict. The British soldiers had received a fair trial, in spite of how unpopular they were. Besides, it seemed that the colonists had won this round of the fight with England. On the same day as the Massacre, Parliament had decided that it would no longer try to collect most of the new taxes! The army was ordered to leave Boston.

Now, life in the city returned almost to normal. Paul went back to making silver. Earlier, he had moved his family to a bigger house on North Square, near the Cockerel Church. The Reveres' new home was considered a "mansion," even though it was really only a little larger than the house on Fish Street. Paul was proud that it had seventeen windows.

Paul hadn't forgotten about politics. In 1771, on the first anniversary of the Massacre, he staged a strange sort of memorial service. At dusk, crowds gathered in the square to watch the show that was being put on in the front windows of the Revere house.

In one window there was a figure called "the ghost of Sneider." Christopher Sneider was a little boy who had been accidentally shot and killed by a British soldier. There was also a paper tower, a smaller version of the one that had burned on the first Liberty Day, in 1765.

A scene in the second window showed the Massacre itself. Figures dressed as British troops stood with their muskets leveled at the spectators. In front of them were the five people who had been killed in the Massacre. They were falling, and blood ran from their wounds.

The third window showed a figure of a woman representing America. One foot rested on the back of a defeated British soldier.

The figures in the windows were probably dummies, like the ones the Sons of Liberty used during their parades. The second scene, especially, sounds gruesome.

But Paul had serious reasons for putting on this strange show. He had a dream that some day all the English colonies would get together and fight for their independence from England. This was considered a radical idea. Now that the British troops were gone, many of Paul's wealthy friends, men like John Hancock and John Adams, were ready to make their peace with Parliament and the English king.

For that matter, it was hard to imagine that the thirteen colonies would ever join together for any reason. The colonies were constantly arguing among themselves. Sometimes they seemed more intent on fighting each other than on fighting England. Only a few dreamers like Paul Revere thought there would ever be a unified country called America.

Nevertheless, according to one of the Boston newspapers, "many Thousands" came to see the exhibit at the Revere house.

Mohawks!

Paul and Sara did not have long to enjoy their new home on North Square. In December of 1772 Sara Revere gave birth to her eighth baby. The little girl, who was called Isanna, was small and sickly. The baby survived, but Sara herself seemed to grow weaker every day. Five months after Isanna was born, Sara died at thirty-seven.

In colonial times, many women died young. They had lots of babies, and if something went wrong there was little that anyone could do to help them. Their husbands usually looked for another wife right away. The men had no choice. Running a home meant hard work, and lots of it. Even doing the laundry was an all-day job. Women boiled water in big kettles, then rubbed and pounded the clothes until they were clean. Many wives also helped their husbands to run the family business. They were busy from morning until night.

Paul loved his family. His wife's death was hard for him. But everyone expected him to find another wife soon. He had seven children at home, including Isanna. Paul's mother still lived with the family, too. She was now very old, and the house was too much for her to handle alone.

By summer, Paul had met someone he wanted to marry. He must have been in love, because he started writing little poems and riddles. One riddle that he wrote hinted at the name of the young lady who was on his mind.

Here's how the riddle went:

> Take three-fourths of a pain that makes traitors confess,
> With three parts of a place which the wicked don't bless.
> Join four-sevenths of an exercise which shopkeepers use.
> And what bad men do, when they good action refuse.
> These four added together, with great care and Will, point out the fair one nearest my heart.

Even though this is a very old-fashioned riddle, it is still possible to figure out the answer. Traitors in those days were put on a device called the *rack* to make them confess. Three-fourths of the word "rack" would yield the letters RAC. The place the wicked don't like is *hell,* and three parts of that word would be the letters HEL. *Walking* was an exercise that shopkeepers got a lot of, and four-sevenths of "walking" could be WALK. A word that means to do wrong is to *err,* and in colonial times this was often spelled just ER. Put all these letters together, and you have the name of the young woman Paul loved: RACHEL WALKER.

Rachel was an ideal match for Paul. She was twenty-seven, which in those days was considered a bit old for getting married. But she didn't mind taking on the job of raising a ready-made family. Unlike some women from working families, she had been to school and knew how to read and write. No matter what troubles came along, Rachel could always cope with them. Best of all, she had a sense of humor. Like Paul, she was a cheerful person. No matter how many worries she had, she never got discouraged.

Rachel needed her natural good cheer, because the first year of her marriage to Paul Revere was very hard. She and Paul got married in September 1773, five months after Sara died. The baby Isanna also died, just three weeks before the wedding.

Then, while Rachel was trying to get used to being the stepmother of six children, trouble between England and the colonies started up all over again.

Just when it seemed that the colonists were getting tired of fighting, Parliament passed another trade law. This time, the English decided that Americans would have to buy *all* their tea from a British firm called the East India Company. There was absolutely nothing wrong with East India tea. It was good, and cheap besides. Still, the law made a lot of the colonists very unhappy.

People who made money by importing—or even smuggling—tea from other countries were especially unhappy. John Hancock was one of those people. He had made a fortune smuggling Dutch tea. Now no grocer would be allowed to sell tea from Holland.

Even people who weren't going to lose any money hated the new law. They felt that a group of strangers far away in England had no business telling them what they could and could not buy. Today it was tea. Tomorrow it would be something else.

The colonists decided that they had to do something.

On the afternoon of November 28, 1773, Paul Revere was at work in his shop when a boy came running in. "The *Dartmouth* is in the harbor," the boy said, gasping for breath. "She is about to tie up at Griffin's Wharf."

This was the news Paul had been waiting for. He leaped into action. Grabbing his musket, he hurried out into the streets. Griffin's Wharf was near the south end of the waterfront, far from Paul's shop. By the time he arrived, other Sons of Liberty were already on the wharf. Paul helped organize a guard of twenty-five armed men to make sure that no one from the ship would set foot on shore.

By dawn the next morning other members of the Sons of Liberty had ridden through the town, tacking up posters that warned of a new threat to freedom:

Friends! Brethren! Countrymen! That worst of plagues ... is now arrived in the harbour ...

What was this terrible plague that had come to town on the *Dartmouth*? Was it some new disease? Or more British soldiers?

Not at all. It was just East India tea, which was in the hold of the ship.

All day long, Paul and the other Sons of Liberty marched up and down the wharf. The ship's crew was so frightened that they didn't dare unload a single spoonful of tea.

But other ships loaded with tea were on their way. The sailors on these ships might not be so easy to scare. A big crowd showed up for a meeting called by Sam Adams at Faneuil Hall. They were trying to figure out what to do next.

First, the people at the meeting voted to send letters to other ports in the area, warning them not to let any ships carrying East India tea dock. Six of the best riders in Boston were picked to deliver the letters. One of the six was Paul Revere. After a long day of marching up and down the wharf, he mounted his horse and rode off to warn the other towns.

When Paul returned to Boston a few days later, the *Dartmouth* was still at Griffin's Wharf. So were two more ships loaded with East India tea. None of them had unloaded its cargo. Sam Adams was still holding meetings, now at the larger Old South Meeting Hall. Thousands of people returned to the hall every day to hear speeches and cheer the Sons of Liberty.

Finally, the owner of the *Dartmouth* decided that he had no choice but to turn his ship around and take the tea back to England. He went off to ask Thomas Hutchinson, who was now governor, for permission to leave. But Hutchinson refused! He was determined to have all the tea unloaded. When word of the governor's decision got back to the meeting hall, Sam Adams rose to speak. "This meeting can do nothing more to save the country," he said.

With this, the meeting broke up. Everyone rushed out into the streets. Adams hadn't said what was going to happen next, but the word was already spreading that anyone who came down to the docks that night would see quite a sight. The Sons of Liberty had a surprise in store.

Shortly after dark, a group of strange-looking men sneaked out the door of the house of Benjamin Edes, one of Paul Revere's close friends. The strangers wore old blankets pinned around their shoulders. Their faces were smeared with red paint and black soot from the chimney.

The group marched toward the docks. On the

way, they ran into other men who were dressed the same way.

"Ugh!" one group said in greeting to the other.

"Ugh!" answered the second group.

Then someone laughed. "Me know you," a voice said.

"Me know *you*," came the answer.

The strange-looking men were supposed to be Mohawk Indians. But no real Indian dressed or talked this way. Their blankets and war paint were disguises.

Within hours, about one hundred and fifty make-believe Mohawks had reached the wharf. Quickly, they divided into three groups, one group going on board each of the three tea ships. Some of the men went below and began hauling wooden crates of tea up onto the decks. One of the Mohawks pulled out an axe from under his blanket. He raised his arm, then brought the axe down on the crate with a loud *thwack*. Several other "Indians" helped him push the crate up over the side of the ship.

Dumping the tea into the harbor took most of the night. While the "Mohawks" worked, they made jokes. "We're making saltwater tea tonight," one man said. Another joke was that Boston Harbor had become the world's largest teapot. For ever afterward, the night's work would be known as "the Boston Tea Party."

By dawn there were tons of loose tea floating on the waters of the harbor. There was so much tea that people miles away saw the brown streaks in the ocean and wondered what they were.

In many ways the Boston Tea Party was like a real party. Thousands of men, women, and even children had gathered on the docks to watch the fun.

But later, when the governor tried to find out who the make-believe Mohawks were, everyone said they hadn't recognized a single one. Supposedly, all of the "Indians" were young men from out of town. They had been chosen so that no one would be able to recognize them and turn them over to the British. But the truth was, many of Boston's leading Sons of Liberty had not been able to resist taking part in the action, too.

Once the tea was dumped into the harbor, Paul Revere's job was just beginning. Out of all the Sons of Liberty, he had been chosen to spread the news to New York and Philadelphia. There was not even time to catch up on his sleep. At dawn, as soon as the work on the ships was done, he saddled his horse and started out.

In 1773, it often took nine days or more to get from Boston to Philadelphia. A horseback rider had to cover more than three hundred and fifty miles on dirt roads. Since it was December, Paul found many of these roads covered with snow and ice. This made the trip even more difficult.

At night, Paul slept in roadside inns. In the morning, he was up with the sun and ready to start out again. If his horse was too tired, he left it behind and rented another from the inn's owner. He covered about sixty miles a day.

Just eleven days later, Paul was back in Boston. Everyone was amazed that he had made the trip there and back so quickly. Best of all, he had good news. The Sons of Liberty's friends in New York and Philadelphia were impressed by his description of Boston's "Tea Party." They promised that they wouldn't accept any East India tea, either.

Paul's Midnight Ride

No one was supposed to know who had planned the Tea Party. But all Boston guessed that it was the work of Paul Revere, Joseph Warren, and the other Sons of Liberty. This group, whose leaders now called themselves the Committee of Correspondence, had started meeting secretly in the back room of the Green Dragon tavern. Within days, a new song was being sung on the streets of Boston:

> Rally Mohawks! bring out your axes.
> And tell King George we'll pay no taxes
>   On his foreign tea! . . .
> Then rally boys, and hasten on
> To meet our chiefs at the Green Dragon.
> Our Warren's there, and bold Revere
> With hands to do, and words to cheer,
>   For Liberty and laws. . . .

Of course, everyone knew that the English Parliament would try to punish Boston for its little "party." Still, people were surprised when they found out just how harsh the punishment was going to be. Parliament ordered that the port of Boston was to be completely closed down! No ships would be allowed in or out of the harbor.

Most people in Boston earned their living from shipping. Closing the port meant that hundreds of men were soon out of work. Soon there was a shortage of food, too. Many families had to depend on charity from the other colonies for their survival.

Even worse, in June of 1774 England sent more troops to make sure the punishment was carried out. This time there were about five thousand soldiers stationed in Boston. Since there were only about fifteen thousand people in the whole city, this was a large number of soldiers.

Some troops were stationed at the fort on Castle Island. Families with extra rooms in their houses were ordered to take in other troops. Some of the soldiers were honest and polite, but others were not very good houseguests. They ate up the best food, stole money, and treated their hosts as if they were a conquered enemy.

This punishment was supposed to make Boston sorry the Tea Party had ever happened. Instead, it convinced the colonists that England would never treat them fairly. People from *all* the colonies agreed that something had to be done. In the fall of 1774, the leaders of each of the thirteen American colonies decided to meet in Philadelphia to plan their next move. This meeting was called the "First Continental Congress."

The Committee of Correspondence chose Paul Revere to carry letters back and forth between them and their representatives in Philadelphia. He always left the city secretly so that the British wouldn't learn of his activities. On these journeys, Paul was more than just a messenger—he told everyone he met how bad things were in Boston. Sooner or later, he said, the colonists would have to go to war to win their freedom from England.

Most of the leaders of the other colonies still thought they could work out their differences with England. But when Paul Revere talked, they listened. Paul had a reputation as a fine silversmith and a solid citizen. They knew his predictions were not just wild talk.

Some people began to prepare for war. Farmers outside of Boston were already hiding supplies of guns and ammunition. The same groups of volunteer soldiers who had once helped the British Army fight France were now getting ready to shoot "Redcoats," as they called British soldiers. These American volunteers were nicknamed the "Minute Men." This was because they were ready to leave their homes and farms and become soldiers on a minute's notice.

But who would give that notice? Who would tell the Minute Men when it was time to start fighting?

In the fall of 1774, Paul Revere and some of the other important "Mechanics" of Boston formed a Watch Committee to spy on the British Army. Members of the committee found out all they could about the army's plans, then passed on the information to Sam Adams, John Hancock, Joseph Warren, and the other members of the group that met at the Green Dragon tavern.

Paul had a network of friends who had ways of finding out the secrets of the British. One of these friends was a bookstore owner named Henry Knox. Knox was six feet, seven inches tall and rather overweight. Despite his large size, many people did not take him seriously.

Henry Knox sold books about military history to many British officers. When the officers came into his shop he would get them into long conversations about the famous battles of history. This friendly young giant seemed so harmless that the British officers saw nothing wrong in discussing their plans with him. They had no idea that every word they said was being repeated in the back room of the Green Dragon.

Unfortunately, the spying worked both ways. Paul's committee had a plan to send out groups of men to follow the British patrols at night. But they soon realized that the British commander, General Gage, knew exactly what they were doing. The only way the British could have known their plans was if someone on the Watch Committee was a traitor. But who?

At the beginning of every meeting, Paul passed a Bible around the room. All the men swore that they would never tell a soul about what went on. But, still, the leaks continued. Paul started to wonder whether the spy might be even one of the top leaders of the Sons of Liberty. He suspected a man named Dr. Church. The doctor was an important member of the Watch Committee, and he was always bragging about how much he hated the British. Nevertheless, he had been seen having dinner with a British officer. When the Sons asked Dr. Church why he was so friendly with the British, Church replied that it was only to get information from them.

Paul found this excuse hard to believe. But he had no proof that Dr. Church was doing anything wrong. Without evidence, he could never convince his friends that such an important man was helping the British.

An emergency arose that made it impossible to investigate Dr. Church, or anyone else, for the time being. In December, Paul's spies learned that General Gage was sending troops to Fort William and Mary in New Hampshire. Paul rode all the way to Portsmouth, some sixty miles, to warn the local Sons of Liberty. The weather was so cold that Paul and his horse nearly froze to death—but they got there in time. The New Hampshire Sons of Liberty captured the fort before General Gage's reinforcements arrived.

Two months later, in February of 1775, Paul and a few other members of his Watch Committee took the risk of rowing out to Castle Island to see what was going on at the fort there. They were caught and thrown into prison. Surprisingly, the British commander let them go after two days. Perhaps he thought that keeping Paul Revere in jail would just make the army more unpopular than it already was.

After that, Boston was quiet for almost two months. Then, early in April, Paul learned that some of the British soldiers had been told that their regular orders were canceled. These soldiers belonged to what was called the "light infantry." They were the best shots and the fastest marchers.

Paul guessed that General Gage was going to send the light infantry to the village of Concord, where the Minute Men had hidden a supply of guns and ammunition. Unfortunately, except for Paul and Joseph Warren, the most important Sons of Liberty were out of town. In fact, Sam Adams and John Hancock happened to be visiting some of Hancock's relatives in the village of Lexington, which was right on the road to Concord.

It was getting harder and harder for Paul to leave Boston without being seen. But Sunday, April 16, was Easter. Paul took advantage of the quiet holiday morning to slip out of town. He went to Concord, where he warned the Minute Men to hide their supply of weapons in the woods.

Paul also stopped in Lexington to talk with Adams and Hancock. John Hancock was on his way to Philadelphia, where the Continental Congress was meeting again. It didn't seem smart to continue his

journey now, when he might run into British soldiers on the road. For the time being, Hancock and Adams decided to stay put in Lexington. Paul promised to ride out there again, when and if he found out more about General Gage's plans.

Paul returned to Boston by a roundabout route, to avoid meeting any British soldiers. He took the road to Charlestown, a finger of land that jutted out into Boston Harbor. From there, he rowed across the water to his own North End neighborhood.

If the British sprang their surprise attack, he wasn't sure he would be able to get out of town again. Just in case he didn't make it, he arranged some secret signals. If the British left Boston by the main road, Paul would arrange to have one lantern hung in the tower of Christ Church. If the soldiers instead took boats, heading up the Charles River, two lanterns would hang in the tower.

As soon as the Charlestown Sons of Liberty saw either of these signals they would know that Paul was on his way. They were to bring a good horse and come down to the place where he planned to dock his rowboat. If Paul didn't show up in half an hour, they could assume that he had been captured or killed. Then someone else would have to ride out from Charlestown to warn the Minute Men in Lexington and Concord.

*　　*　　*

Shortly before ten o'clock on the night of April 18, 1775, a messenger knocked on Paul's door to tell him that the British troops were about to make their move. A Sons of Liberty spy had learned that as many as a thousand soldiers were going to be loaded on boats and sent up the Charles River. The soldiers should arrive in Lexington by dawn the next morning.

Joseph Warren had already ordered a man named Billy Dawes to ride to Lexington and Concord by way of the main road out of Boston. This was the most direct route—but the British were sure to be guarding the road. What if Dawes didn't get through? As an added safeguard, Paul decided to try the plan that he had worked out with the Sons of Liberty in Charlestown.

First, Paul hurried off to meet Robert Newman, the man who was to set up the lantern signals in the church spire.

Unfortunately, there was a group of British officers living in Newman's house. Of course, the officers had no idea that they were staying in the home of one of the rebels. Newman had seen troops in the street, and he knew something was up. But how was he going to get away from his house without making the officers suspicious?

Newman pretended to be sleepy. He told the officers that he was going up to bed early. Then he crawled out of an upstairs window and inched his way across the roof.

When Paul arrived, Robert Newman was already waiting in the street. "The signal is two lanterns," Paul said.

Newman let himself into Christ Church and hurried up the wooden stairs of the tower. Above him in the darkness were the dim outlines of the church's eight huge bells. These were the same bells that Paul had rung as a teenager. But now, the last thing Newman wanted was to set the bells ringing and attract attention. Carefully, he made his way up past the bells to the little platform in the highest part of the church spire. He lit a pair of lanterns and set them in the window.

Paul, meanwhile, had gone home to get his riding boots and jacket. North Square was full of soldiers, but, fortunately, no one recognized the rebel express rider, Paul Revere. Paul changed his clothes and hurried to the waterfront where two more Sons of Liberty were waiting to row him across to Charlestown.

The boatmen warned Paul that the British warship *Somerset* was anchored right near the mouth of the river. They were afraid that sentries on the *Somerset* would hear the noise made by the squeaky oars of the little rowboat.

Quickly, they came up with a plan. One of the men had a girlfriend who lived nearby. He ran to her house, stood in the shadows under her bedroom window, and whistled. The young woman came right to the window. When she heard the problem, she pulled off her flannel petticoat and threw it down to him.

The boatmen tore the petticoat in half and tied the pieces around the oars to muffle the sound. But they still weren't ready to shove off. Paul was so nervous that he had forgotten to bring his spurs! According to the story Paul told years later, his loyal dog had followed him down to the water's edge. Paul wrote a note to Rachel and tied it to the dog's collar. The dog ran off, and returned minutes later carrying his spurs.

Finally, they were ready to leave. Paul jumped into the boat. Just around the point, the first barges loaded with British troops were already in the water. Much closer, Paul could see the black hull of the *Somerset*. The boatmen headed out into the harbor, staying as far as possible from the great ship.

The moon was rising. It was much easier to see than it had been just an hour earlier. Paul and the boatmen had a good view of the *Somerset*, as it listed in the stiff breeze. They were sure that at any minute one of the sailors on the ship would spot them. If the *Somerset* fired off one of its big guns, their little boat would be blown right out of the water.

But luckily no one noticed the rowboat. Minutes later, it reached the other side of the Charles River.

The Charlestown Sons of Liberty had seen Newman's lanterns. A Colonel Conant was waiting with a horse that he had borrowed from a rich farmer. Paul had ridden lots of good horses as an express rider, but this was one of the best he had ever seen.

Unfortunately, Conant also had some bad news. The British were watching the road out of Charlestown, too.

Today, Charlestown is home to many thousands of people. But in 1775, it was still a small village. Minutes after leaving Conant, Paul found himself on a lonely country road. Next to the road were open fields called the Charlestown Commons. This was the place where condemned criminals were hanged. Paul knew that if he were caught, the British would treat him as a criminal, too.

Seconds after he passed the hanging grounds, Paul realized he was not alone. Up ahead he could see two men on horseback, hiding in the shadow of a big tree. The men were British sentries. Years later, he would still have a vivid memory of this moment. "I was near enough to see their holsters," he wrote.

The sentries had already spotted him. One started toward him, while the other pursued him down the road, waiting to catch Paul if he managed to slip past his partner. Paul didn't hesitate. He turned his horse abruptly and galloped off across the Commons. The sentry who was nearer started to chase him.

Paul dug in his spurs, and his horse picked up speed. The sentry tried to catch up, but his horse just wasn't fast enough. Before they had reached the other side of the Commons, the sentry gave up.

Paul soon made his way back to the main road. Fortunately, his horse was as strong as it was fast. The hard chase didn't tire the animal out. For more than an hour, his horse ran as fast as it could.

Paul passed through several small villages on his way to Lexington. At each one, he slowed down just long enough to bang on doors and shout his warning. "The Redcoats are coming!" Villagers woke up and looked out their windows just in time to see Paul rush headlong into the darkness.

Shortly after midnight Paul reached Lexington. The first thing he did was go to the house where Sam Adams and John Hancock were staying. It was already so late that everyone had gone to bed. Paul banged on the door.

Eight men who had been assigned to guard Adams and Hancock were sleeping downstairs in the house. One of them got up and came to the door. "The family has just retired," he said. "Not so much noise."

"Noise!" shouted Paul. "You'll have noise enough before long. The regulars are coming out." The regulars were the British soldiers.

John Hancock heard the commotion. Going to

his bedroom window, he shouted, "Come in, Revere. We are not afraid of you."

One of the guards ran off to ring the church bell. All over Lexington, families struggled out of bed and lit their candles. Men and boys grabbed their rifles and muskets and rushed to the village square. Within an hour there were about one hundred thirty Minute Men waiting in the square. They marched up and down, trying to keep up their courage.

A little before 1:00 A.M., Billy Dawes, the other messenger from Boston, showed up. Like Paul, Dawes had managed to get past the British sentries. But even though he had left Boston first, it had taken him longer to get to Lexington.

Someone still had to warn the village of Concord, six miles away. Paul and Billy Dawes decided to ride to Concord together. Setting out, on their way past the village church, they ran into another man, Dr. Samuel Prescott. Prescott lived in Concord, but he had been visiting his sweetheart in Lexington. He volunteered to ride with them.

Revere, Dawes, and Prescott had made it about halfway to Concord, when suddenly, with no warning at all, a group of British officers came rushing out into the road. The soldiers and their leader, Major Mitchell, had been hiding in the woods, waiting to ambush anyone who came along.

Dr. Prescott had an advantage. He was near home, and even though it was dark he knew his way around. He aimed his horse for a stone wall and urged it to jump. The horse leaped over the wall, and Prescott disappeared into the darkness.

Prescott made it all the way to Concord. He woke up the village and warned everyone. By morning, the Minute Men had safely hidden their stash of weapons. Some of it they buried in the fields. One farmer even buried several cannons so the British couldn't capture them.

Billy Dawes, meanwhile, had tried to follow Dr. Prescott. But Dawes's horse refused to jump the wall. It reared back on its hind legs, causing Dawes to fall out of the saddle. With several British officers bearing down on him, he sprinted for the woods and escaped.

Paul never had a chance to get away. He had been riding in front, a few yards ahead of his companions. Before he could reach the wall, he was surrounded by ten soldiers on horseback.

Major Mitchell threatened Paul with a pistol. "If you go an inch farther you are a dead man," he warned.

Then, more politely, the major asked, "Sir, may I crave your name?"

"My name is Revere," said Paul.

When Mitchell heard the name, he realized that he had captured one of the leaders of the Sons of Liberty. He could hardly believe his good luck. "What!" he said. *"Paul* Revere?"

"Yes," admitted Paul.

At this, all the soldiers started swearing. They called Paul a "rebel" and many names worse than that. The major pulled out his pistol and held it against Paul's head. "If you do not tell the truth, I'll blow your brains out," he promised.

"I call myself a man of truth," Paul said calmly. He told Major Mitchell that capturing him wouldn't do any good. The whole countryside was already "alarmed." The British surprise had been spoiled.

One of the officers had grabbed the reins of Paul's horse. "We are now going towards your friends," Mitchell said. "If you attempt to run, or we are insulted, we will blow your brains out."

The British started back in the direction of Lexington with Paul as their prisoner. The soldier who was leading Paul's horse leaned over and whispered to him, "You're in a critical situation."

Paul didn't have to be told this. As far as the British were concerned, the Sons of Liberty were traitors. If he were turned over to General Gage, he would be tried for treason. He could well end up hanging on Charlestown Commons.

Back in Lexington, the Minute Men were still marching up and down in the dark, waiting for the British. They were getting more excited by the minute. Several of the men started firing their rifles into the air.

Major Mitchell and his group heard the shots. It sounded as if the battle had already started. Mitchell was in such a hurry to join the fighting that he lost interest in his prisoner. He ordered Paul to get down from his horse, then told his sergeant to take Paul's good horse and let his own run off.

Major Mitchell promised Paul that the sergeant would be borrowing his horse only "for the night." But, of course, he had no intention of keeping his word. This was one borrowed horse that was most unlikely to be returned. Paul Revere never saw the brave animal again.

The Shot Heard Around the World

Paul was lucky to be alive. But he wasn't out of danger yet. He couldn't afford to stay on the road. The next British patrol to come along might not be so quick to let him go.

Paul took off through the woods, heading in the general direction of Lexington. He was still wearing his spurs, so it wasn't easy climbing over stone walls and cutting through the underbrush in the dark. Very soon, he was lost. Just when he was getting discouraged, he nearly tripped over a tombstone. He realized that he was in the Lexington cemetery, very close to the house where John Hancock and Sam Adams had been staying.

Paul had risked his life in order to warn Hancock and Adams to get out of Lexington. But strangely enough, when Paul arrived back at the house, both men were still inside. John Hancock was a clever man, but he had problems making up his mind. He had wasted the hour or two since Paul's arrival arguing.

First, Hancock had insisted that he wanted to stay and fight along with the Minute Men. Sam Adams thought that this was a crazy idea. The colonists were outnumbered ten to one. He told Hancock that he was too valuable to be captured at the very beginning of a war. The Boston patriots were counting on Hancock to go down to Philadelphia, to represent them in Congress. It would be his job to convince the Congress to send an army to help drive the British out of Boston.

Besides arguing with Sam Adams, Hancock was having problems with his fiancée, Dolly Quincy. Dolly and Hancock's aunt had come out to Lexington for a visit. Poor Dolly had been trying to get Hancock to marry her for three years. He *said* he wanted to marry her, but he kept backing out at the last minute. Now Dolly realized that if war broke out, she might not be able to get home to Boston— she might be separated from her family for years.

Dolly was very unhappy. Her argument with Hancock went on and on. By now it was after 3:00 A.M. Finally, Paul and the eight guards managed to hustle Hancock and Adams into a carriage. Paul rode with them to Woburn, a village away from the main road. The British would have a harder time finding them there.

Hancock was safe for the time being. But now he brought up another problem. In all the excitement of arguing with Dolly and Sam Adams he had left his trunk behind. The trunk was full of letters and papers that he was taking with him to Philadelphia. The secret plans of the Sons of Liberty and the Boston committees were in those papers—and the names of all the members, too. And even worse, Hancock had left the trunk in the local tavern, rather than in the house where he had been staying. There was a good chance that the British soldiers would stop at the Lexington tavern. What if they found the trunk?

Rescuing John Hancock was turning out to be more trouble than Paul had bargained for. Riding another borrowed horse, he headed back to Lexington for the third time that night. Paul found the trunk in the upstairs room of the tavern. He was trying to figure out how to move it, when he heard the sound of drums in the distance. Peering out the window he saw red-coated soldiers coming down the road. The British had arrived!

It was dawn, and down on the village green the Minute Men were still waiting. "Don't fire unless fired upon," their captain ordered.

Paul asked one of the men in the tavern to help him move the heavy trunk. They got it down the stairs and started across the village green, right past the rebel soldiers. It was impossible to run with the trunk between them, but Paul and his helper moved as fast as they could. They scurried across the green and disappeared into some bushes.

Suddenly, a shot rang out. "I heard the report and turned my head," Paul remembered many years later. But he couldn't tell who had fired.

Back on the green, the British captain heard the shot and gave the order to his troops to fire back. Eight Minute Men were killed; ten more were wounded.

The shooting didn't last long before the Minute Men dispersed. And soon after, the British officers, having lost just one soldier, ordered their men to march straight to Concord. Despite all the trouble Paul had taken to move the trunk, the soldiers didn't bother to stop at the Lexington tavern.

The British soldiers were feeling sure of themselves. Their red coats still looked as spiffy as ever. Their steel bayonets sparkled in the early morning sun. The drummers and flute players marching at the head of the column struck up a sprightly march tune. One of the soldiers thought he had never heard such "grand music."

But the British were in for a big surprise. By now Paul Revere's warning had spread to all the villages for miles around. One group of Minute Men was waiting at a bridge outside Concord. Hundred of others had grabbed their guns and were hiding behind trees and stone walls all along the road from Lexington to Boston. When the British were forced to retreat from Concord and tried to march back to Boston, the Americans started taking random shots at them. One by one the Redcoats were picked off.

The British were so angry that they started setting fire to houses along the road. But there was nothing they could do to stop the Minute Men from shooting at them. At every turn in the road there was another ambush waiting for the soldiers. Since the rebels hid behind fences and trees, the soldiers could not see them well enough to fight back effectively. And they didn't know the land nearly as well as the rebels who had lived there all their lives.

There were no more proud march tunes now. Scared and exhausted, the British hurried back toward the safety of Boston. Everyone was on foot, even the officers. All the horses were being used to carry the wounded.

The wonderful British Army had been run off by a bunch of farmers! This just wasn't supposed to happen. The British had lost this one battle. But even so, many of the king's officers felt sure that the Americans would be beaten in a matter of days.

But Paul Revere and the other Sons of Liberty were in no mood to surrender. They weren't going to give up until America was free and independent.

Years later, some people who were in Lexington on April 19, 1775, said that the first shot fired that morning came from the upstairs room of the tavern—the very place where, minutes earlier, Paul Revere had been struggling with John Hancock's trunk. But if Paul had any idea who fired the shot, he never said.

Who fired first really didn't matter anymore. What mattered was that the shot that rang out in Lexington would change history. People called it "the shot heard around the world."

The American Revolution had begun. At first,

Paul Revere, Sam Adams, and the other Boston leaders weren't sure what to do. John Hancock hurried down to Philadelphia to ask Congress for help.

Boston was now under the complete control of the British. Joseph Warren, Dr. Church, and a few other rebels managed to escape from the city. But Robert Newman, the man who had hung the lanterns in the church tower, was placed under arrest. Paul was very worried about the Revere family. He was afraid that Rachel and the children would try to leave the city to join him. If they were caught, they might be arrested, too.

For the time being, the Committee of Safety was hiding out in the town of Cambridge, just outside of Boston. On Friday, two days after the fight at Lexington, the committee was holding a meeting when Dr. Church made a surprise announcement. "I am determined to go to Boston tomorrow," he told the group.

"Are you serious?" asked Warren. "They will hang you if they catch you in Boston."

But Dr. Church insisted that he was willing to take the risk. The wounded Minute Men needed medicine. He was going to sneak into the city and bring some back.

Paul had been suspicious of Dr. Church for a long time. But now he had changed his mind. When Dr. Church had shown up in Cambridge, the stockings he was wearing were spattered with blood. The doctor had told everyone that he had taken part in the attack on the British soldiers. He said that the man standing next to him had been shot and killed. The man's blood had gotten on his stockings.

This story made a big impression on Paul. He figured that if Dr. Church had been that close to the fighting he couldn't be a traitor. So Paul asked the doctor to take a message to Rachel. He warned her to stay where she was for the time being. He also asked her to send him some money.

The next day, an official from one of the Boston churches happened to go to General Gage's house to deliver a message. While he was waiting to see the general, the man was very surprised to see Gage come out of his office with Dr. Church. The two men seemed to be old friends.

But the men in Cambridge had no way of knowing about this meeting. When Dr. Church got back to Cambridge he told a story of a narrow escape from Boston. He said that he had been stopped by a British patrol and taken to Gage's house to be questioned. After a while, Dr. Church said, Gage let him go, but only on the condition that he leave Boston right away.

Paul and the other committee members believed Dr. Church's story. Months went by before they learned what had really happened. Dr. Church had taken the answer Rachel wrote to Paul's letter and given it to General Gage. He took the money that Rachel sent, too. Church had been spying for the British all along!

Dr. Church was sentenced to jail. Later, the Americans freed him in exchange for an American who was a prisoner of the British.

Throughout the colonies, families were choosing up sides. Many colonists were still loyal to King George III and Parliament, even in the villages around Lexington and Concord. These people were eager to move to Boston, where the British Army could protect them. And of course, Boston families who were loyal to the American patriots were just as eager to get out of the city.

Several weeks after the fighting started, the British let some civilians change sides. Even so, General Gage wasn't about to do any favors for the family of the famous express rider, Paul Revere—his family would have to stay. Paul solved the problem by bribing a British officer. In return for a few sides of beef and some beer, the officer allowed the Revere family to leave Boston. Rachel, the children, and Paul's mother piled a few belongings on a wagon and started for Watertown, a town to the west of Boston. This had become the new capital of the Massachusetts rebels.

The only member of the family to stay behind was Paul's oldest son, Paul Jr. He was left in Boston to guard the house and the shop. Paul Jr. was only fifteen years old, and protecting the family's property was a big responsibility. But he managed to keep the house from being destroyed.

Paul himself continued to carry messages for the rebel committees. But he soon had an even more important job. Americans no longer wanted to use British money—they wanted to have their own. Since Paul knew how to make engravings, he was asked to print the first money for the Colony of Massachusetts.

First, Paul had to arrange for his copper plates and tools to be smuggled out of Boston. Then he had a terrible time finding paper. The only kind he could get was almost as thick as cardboard. Some colonists laughed at the strange-looking money, but it was the best Paul could do. And it wasn't British— that was the important thing.

While Paul was busy printing money, volunteers from all over New England had come to the areas near Boston to help fight the British. Down in Philadelphia, John Hancock and Sam and John Adams convinced Congress to organize the volunteer soldiers into an army that represented all thirteen American colonies. This was called the Continental Army.

But who would head the army? Hancock secretly thought that Congress ought to make him the general in charge. Wasn't he the richest man in Boston, the town where the fighting had started? But Congress had other ideas. It voted to put the new army under the command of a Virginian named George Washington. Even Hancock's best friends were relieved. Washington was an experienced soldier—he had fought with the British in the war against France, and proved himself a hero. Hancock did not have nearly as much experience at war.

It was hard to imagine that anyone, even George Washington, could drive the British out of Boston. But Washington figured out a plan. By the spring of 1776, his army had surrounded the city. The British realized that they were trapped. Their troops were loaded onto ships, and on March 17, they sailed away from Boston.

The Revolutionary War was really just getting started. It would continue for seven more years. The British would capture New York, and march across New Jersey to Philadelphia. There would be fighting in Virginia, too, and in the colonies farther south, until a peace treaty was signed in 1783. But Boston was back in the hands of the Americans for good.

Many changes had occurred among the Sons of Liberty. Everyone had expected that brave, handsome Joseph Warren would become a hero. Warren was made a general in the army. But he had died in the first big battle of the war, at Bunker Hill. He had never even had a chance to get himself a uniform.

Surprisingly, the Boston patriot who did become a war hero was Henry Knox, the mild-mannered bookstore owner who had spied for the colonists. Knox too was appointed a general, one of Washington's favorites.

Paul Revere ended up in the Continental Army, too. He was made a colonel. After the British sailed away from Boston, he was put in charge of the Castle Island fort, the very place where he had once been a prisoner.

Colonel Revere's big chance to get involved in the fighting came in 1779. The British had set up a small new fort at a place called Castine, on the Maine coast. The Americans decided to send twelve hundred soldiers to conquer the fort. A number of ships were supposed to help by attacking Castine from the sea. Massachusetts sent its entire navy—all three ships. The brand-new Continental Navy sent three more ships. Other boats that belonged to private individuals went along, too.

Paul started off with high hopes. But from the first day, things started going wrong. Paul did not think much of the major who was leading the march. To make things worse, many of Paul's soldiers were just boys, with no training at all. As soon as there was any trouble, quite a few of them ran away from the fighting.

In the meantime, the general of the army troops and the commander of the navy ships kept arguing about who should attack first. They were still arguing when four British warships sailed into the harbor and set several of the American ships on fire. That put an end to the American plan. The soldiers on shore ran for their lives.

Paul and his men had to hike all the way back to Boston. But Paul's troubles weren't over yet. As soon as he was back home, he learned that he had been charged with cowardice and disobedience!

Not one of the charges was true. The real problem was that Paul wasn't used to taking orders. If he thought another officer was stupid or dishonest, he said so. But he never disobeyed orders, and he certainly had not acted cowardly. In fact, he had gotten very angry with the soldiers who *had* tried to run away.

General Ward didn't believe the charges against Paul. He was ready to forget all about them.

But Paul was outraged. He demanded a trial "where I can meet my accusers face to face."

It took two years for Paul to get his trial. The war with Britain was finally coming to an end, and now that there was good news to celebrate, no one but Paul really cared much about what had happened up in Maine. France had come into the war on the American side, and down in the southern colonies the British general, Cornwallis, had run into trouble. In October of 1781, the Americans and the French trapped Cornwallis's army at Yorktown, Virginia, and the British general was forced to surrender.

Four months later, in February of 1782, the

army finally got around to Paul's court-martial. Thirteen officers were appointed to hear the case. But by this time, Paul's accusers must have had second thoughts. Some of them didn't even show up to testify, and the court found Paul innocent.

Even though the charges against Paul were false, they probably ended any chance of his getting an important job in the government after the war. But he didn't seem to mind. He was happy that his reputation had been cleared. The war was almost over by now, and he was eager to go back to his old life—to Rachel, his children, and the shop where he made beautiful silver teapots, bowls, and cups.

Paul Revere, Businessman

In 1788, four and a half years after the war had ended, Paul attended one last meeting at the Green Dragon tavern. This time, the meeting was not held in secret. All the "Mechanics" of Boston were invited, and so many showed up that the tavern could not hold them all. The crowd spilled out into the streets.

The meeting had been called to discuss the new Constitution that had been written in Philadelphia by the leaders of the thirteen colonies. Should Massachusetts vote to accept the Constitution? Should it become part of the new nation, the United States of America?

The group inside the Green Dragon knew what they wanted. The vote was unanimous. Every single person there voted yes. The crowd in the street was overjoyed. Everyone gave three cheers for the new Constitution!

But one important person was missing from the meeting. It was old Sam Adams, who had started the Sons of Liberty so many years before. Sam Adams was disappointed by the way the Revolution had turned out. He had dreamed that once

America was free, there would be no more divisions between rich and poor.

Of course, it had not turned out that way. Many of the Sons of Liberty had been killed or wounded in the war. Others had lost all their property. At the same time, some people who had stayed in Boston and done business with the British were now rich. This was unfair, and it made Sam Adams bitterly unhappy. No one was sure whether he would support the Constitution or not.

The group at the Green Dragon decided to send a committee to talk to Adams. It chose Paul Revere as its spokesman. No one knows exactly what Paul said to his old friend. One story about the meeting is that Sam Adams asked how many people had shown up to vote yes. "More than there are stars in the sky," Paul is supposed to have said.

Whatever Paul told Sam Adams, it was convincing. Adams voted in favor of the Constitution, and Massachusetts became part of the United States.

Unlike Sam Adams, Paul did not waste any time worrying about how things might have been. It certainly didn't bother him that there were still wealthy people in Boston. Paul's head was filled with ideas for getting rich himself.

The old Liberty Tree was long gone. The British had cut it down while they were in control of the city. But Paul had opened up a new shop across from where the famous tree had stood. The shop sold many things besides silver, such as writing papers, wallpaper, pencils, eyeglasses, playing cards, and even wigs.

Paul's plan for making money included other ventures, too. At the beginning of the war, one of the big problems of the army had been that not a single person in the colonies knew how to make cannons. Paul had given this a lot of thought. While the war was still going on he had started to learn how to make cannons from a French officer who had come to help the American Army.

Now Paul started reading everything he could about the science of metalworking. Before long, he had his own factory on the outskirts of Boston. All kinds of iron hardware were made there. Soon, the factory was turning out things made from copper and brass, too—including cannons.

When the United States Navy ordered its first new ships, Paul supplied the copper and brass parts. The Revere Works became the first factory in America to make the sheets of copper that could be nailed to the sides of wooden ships to protect them from cannon shot. Paul's factory also made copper roofs for many important buildings, including the State House in Boston and City Hall in New York.

But the metalworking project closest to Paul's heart was learning to make bells. Paul had loved bells ever since he was a boy. But nearly all the bells in America had been made in Europe. And the few made in the colonies had not been very good. Paul wanted his country to be able to make bells it could be proud of.

It was very hard to make a good bell. The bell-maker had to use the right combination of metals. He had to fill the huge molds quickly with the melted metal, or the bell wouldn't sound right. Expert bellmakers didn't like to pass on their secrets, so Paul and his helpers had to learn many tricks on their own, by trial and error.

Paul tried casting his first bell in 1792. It was made from over nine hundred pounds of molten metal. The mold was so big that the workers had to dig a huge pit in the ground to hold it!

When the bell was finished, some people complained that it had a "panny" sound. Whatever that meant, it can't have been good. But Paul was not too disappointed. He was proud that the bell worked at all. He had an inscription cut into the rim: "The first bell cast in Boston. 1792. P. Revere."

Paul kept studying the art of bellmaking. Eventually, he made about four hundred bells. His bells hung in churches and schools all over New England and America. A few of them still exist.

Besides making bells and hardware and copper for ships, Paul still kept his silversmith's shop. By now, he was one of the best silversmiths in America—each piece he made was a work of art. Even today, Paul Revere's silver is collected by people who love beautiful things. You can see his work

in many museums, and in picture books about fine silver.

Within a few years, the Reveres were able to move from North Square to a much larger, finer house. For once, they had plenty of room. They even had their own stable in the back yard.

Paul was very well off, but he never became as rich as he might have. The reason was that Paul liked giving money away as much as he liked making it.

By now, he had a very large family. Paul still had six living children from his marriage to Sara. He and Rachel had eight more children. Three of these children died as babies, but the rest lived to grow up. That meant that Paul had eleven grown children in all. And even then, the Revere family kept expanding. Paul Jr. had seven children. Deborah, Paul's oldest daughter, married a man named Amos Lincoln, a distant cousin of Abraham Lincoln's father. Amos and Deborah had nine children. Then Deborah died and Amos married her younger sister Betty, and they had four *more* children. There would soon be other grandchildren, too.

Paul was a very generous father. Even when his children were grown, they knew they could turn to their father for help if they needed money.

Paul also helped out his grandchildren and his nieces and nephews. He was even loyal to old customers who had fallen on hard times. Sometimes he made silver for them even though he knew they would never pay their bills.

From time to time, he and Rachel took in people whom no one else would. One winter, a woman appeared in Boston who had run away from her husband and was expecting a baby by another man. The woman had been a minister's wife, so this was considered very shocking behavior. Good church members refused to speak to her; they even talked about driving her out of town. Paul and Rachel Revere came to the woman's rescue. They let her live in their home until after the baby was born.

Paul helped lots of other people, too. His desk was piled high with letters from people asking him for favors. He almost always said yes.

When Paul was an old man he tried his hand at writing poetry. In one long poem, he listed all the things that made him happy. The list included his dear wife, his friends, and horseback riding. He also wrote about waking up in the morning to the sweet song of a yellow bird singing in his garden. But the thing that made him most happy was work. "*Labour*, and *Health* go hand in hand," he wrote. "I *exercise* prefer to *wealth*."

One thing Paul didn't mention in his poem was that he had been a hero. He hadn't forgotten his marvelous midnight ride, but he preferred to let others do his bragging for him. Already, a poet named Ebenezer Stiles had tried to tell the story of the ride in verse. Poor Mr. Stiles got nearly all the facts wrong, however—he thought that Paul and his horse had swum across the Charles River! He also thought Paul had got as far as Concord, not just Lexington. He even pictured Paul standing on the Concord Green making a long-winded speech.

Paul Revere lived to be eighty-three years old. Exercise must have really worked for him because when he died, in 1818, the newspapers all mentioned that he was an "early Patriot" who had never been sick a day in his life. But despite Mr. Stiles's poem—or maybe because of it—the authors of the newspaper stories weren't sure just what this "early Patriot" had done during the years just before the Revolution.

Paul had never asked for any thanks for all he had done to help free America from British rule. He didn't really become famous until long after his death. In 1861, Henry Wadsworth Longfellow wrote his poem "Paul Revere's Ride." Like Mr. Stiles, Longfellow got a few facts wrong. But he had the spirit right. His poem, which quickly became very popular, appears at the end of this book.

In 1875, Boston decided to celebrate the one hundredth anniversary of the Battle of Lexington. The celebration was held at Christ Church, whose name had by then been changed to Old North Church. The church was packed with spectators who had come for the occasion. Robert Newman's son, now a very old man, had been chosen to carry "Paul Revere's lanterns." When Mr. Newman brought the lighted lanterns down the aisle, on his way to carry them up into the tower, everyone in the church cheered. The noise was so loud it "made the house rock."

No doubt Paul Revere, who had rung the bells of Christ Church so many years before, would have thought that the cheers were the best thank-yous of all.

Highlights in the Life of

PAUL REVERE

January 1, 1735

On this day Paul Revere is baptized at the Cockerel Church. This date is usually called Paul's birthday, but he may actually have been born on the previous day.

For that matter, when Paul was very young he would have celebrated his baptism day on December 22. When Paul was still a boy, the American colonies decided to change their calendars to make them more accurate. Ten days were added to all dates in the winter months. This changed Paul's baptism day from December 22, 1734, to January 1, 1735.

August 17, 1757

Paul marries Sara Orne.

March 5, 1770

British soldiers fire into a crowd, killing five people. This event becomes known as the Boston Massacre.

May 3, 1773

Sara Revere dies at the age of thirty-seven. Sara was the mother of eight children, seven of whom are still living at the time of her death. The baby, Isanna, dies four months later.

October 10, 1773

Paul marries his second wife, Rachel Walker. Rachel and Paul will eventually have another eight children.

December 16–17, 1773

The Boston Tea Party. Sons of Liberty disguised as Indians dump 90,000 pounds of tea in Boston Harbor. Paul is chosen to ride to New York and Philadelphia with news of the event.

April 18–19, 1775

Paul Revere's "Midnight Ride" warns the countryside that the British Army is on its way.

1792

Paul casts his first bell.

June 26, 1813

Rachel Walker Revere dies at the age of sixty-eight.

May 10, 1818

Paul Revere dies at the age of eighty-three.

Paul Revere's Ride

Listen, my children, and you shall hear
Of the midnight ride of Paul Revere,
On the eighteenth of April, in Seventy-five;
Hardly a man is now alive
Who remembers that famous day and year.

He said to his friend, "If the British march
By land or sea from town to-night,
Hang a lantern aloft in the belfry arch
Of the North Church tower as a signal light,—
One, if by land, and two, if by sea;
And I on the opposite shore will be,
Ready to ride and spread the alarm
Through every Middlesex village and farm,
For the country folk to be up and to arm."

Then he said, "Good night," and with a muffled oar
Silently rowed to the Charlestown shore,
Just as the moon rose over the bay,
When swinging wide at her moorings lay
The Somerset, British man-of-war;
A phantom ship, with each mast and spar
Across the moon like a prison bar,
And a huge black hulk, that was magnified
By its own reflection in the tide.

Meanwhile, his friend, through alley and street,
Wanders and watches with eager ears.
Till in the silence around him he hears

The muster of men at the barrack door,
The sound of arms, and the tramp of feet,
And the measured tread of the grenadiers,
Marching down to their boats on the shore.
Then he climbed the tower of the Old North Church,
By the wooden stairs, with stealthy tread,
To the belfry-chamber overhead,
And startled the pigeons from their perch
On the sombre rafters, that round him made
Masses and moving shapes of shade,—
By the trembling ladder, steep and tall,
To the highest window in the wall,
Where he paused to listen and look down
A moment on the roofs of the town,
And the moonlight flowing over all.

Beneath, in the churchyard, lay the dead,
In their night-encampment on the hill,
Wrapped in silence so deep and still
That he could hear, like a sentinel's tread,
The watchful night-wind, as it went
Creeping along from tent to tent,
And seeming to whisper, "All is well!"
A moment only he feels the spell
Of the place and the hour, and the secret dread
Of the lonely belfry and the dead;
For suddenly all his thoughts are bent
On a shadowy something far away,
Where the river widens to meet the bay,—
A line of black that bends and floats
On the rising tide, like a bridge of boats.

Meanwhile, impatient to mount and ride,
Booted and spurred, with a heavy stride
On the opposite shore walked Paul Revere.
Now he patted his horse's side,
Now gazed at the landscape far and near,

Then, impetuous, stamped the earth,
And turned and tightened his saddle-girth;

But mostly he watched with eager search
The belfry-tower of the Old North Church,
As it rose above the graves on the hill,
Lonely and spectral and sombre and still.
And lo! as he looks, on the belfry's height
A glimmer, and then a gleam of light!
He springs to the saddle, the bridle he turns,
But lingers and gazes, till full on his sight
A second lamp in the belfry burns!

A hurry of hoofs in a village street,
A shape in the moonlight, a bulk in the dark,
And beneath, from the pebbles, in passing, a spark
Struck out by a steed flying fearless and fleet:
That was all! And yet, through the gloom and the light,
The fate of a nation was riding that night;
And the spark struck out by that steed, in his flight,
Kindled the land into flame with its heat.

He has left the village and mounted the steep,
And beneath him, tranquil and broad and deep,
Is the Mystic, meeting the ocean tides;
And under the alders that skirt its edge,
Now soft on the sand, now loud on the ledge,
Is heard the tramp of his steed as he rides.

It was twelve by the village clock,
When he crossed the bridge into Medford town.
He heard crowing of the cock,
And the barking of the farmer's dog,
And felt the damp of the river fog,
That rises after the sun goes down.

It was one by the village clock,
When he galloped into Lexington.
He saw the gilded weathercock

Swim in the moonlight as he passed,
And the meeting-house windows, blank and bare,
Gaze at him with a spectral glare,
As if they already stood aghast
At the bloody work they would look upon.

It was two by the village clock,
When he came to the bridge in Concord town.
He heard the bleating of the flock,
And the twitter of the birds among the trees,
And felt the breath of the morning breeze
Blowing over the meadows brown.
And one was safe and asleep in his bed
Who at the bridge would be first to fall,
Who that day would be lying dead,
Pierced by a British musket-ball.

You know the rest. In the books you have read,
How the British Regulars fired and fled,—
How the farmers gave them ball for ball,
From behind each fence and farm-yard wall,
Chasing the red-coats down the lane,
Then crossing the fields to emerge again
Under the trees at the turn of the road,
And only pausing to fire and load.

So through the night rode Paul Revere;
And so through the night went his cry of alarm
To every Middlesex village and farm,—
A cry of defiance and not of fear,
A voice in the darkness, a knock at the door,
And a word that shall echo forevermore!
For, borne on the night-wind of the Past,
Through all our history, to the last,
In the hour of darkness and peril and need,
The people will waken and listen to hear
The hurrying hoof-beats of that steed,
And the midnight message of Paul Revere.